Photo credit: Camilla Duffy

Lizz Murphy is an Irish-Australian poet who writes mainly while on the road between Binalong NSW and Canberra ACT, a habit which began while commuting by bus aeons ago. Now she commutes from Binalong to Canberra part-time by car still keeping her eye out for poems. She writes in a variety of styles from prose poetry to micro poetry, sometimes incorporating found text and image.

Lizz has had 14 books published. *The Wear of My Face* is her ninth poetry title. She is widely published in anthologies and journals in Australia and overseas. She is a former *Canberra Times* Poetry Editor and has worked in regional arts development, and as a publicist in arts and publishing. She was once a regional newspaper editor and once upon a time long before that, a shop assistant. Lizz Murphy lives and writes on unceded Ngunnawal Country and blogs occasionally at *A Poet's Slant*.

lizzmurphypoet.blogspot.com

Other works by Lizz Murphy

Poetry
Shebird (2016)
Portrait: 54 Poems (2013)
Six Hundred Dollars (2010)
Walk the Wildly (2009/2017)
Stop Your Cryin (2007)
Two Lips Went Shopping (2000)
Pearls and Bullets (1997)
Do Fish Get Seasick: A Collection of Damn Bus Poems (1994)

Anthologies
The Pearly Griffin: The Story of the Old Griffin Centre
(Co-editor with Sarah St Vincent Welch, 2007)
Everyone Needs Cleaners, Eh! (1997)
Eat the Ocean (1997)
Wee Girls: Women Writing from an Irish Perspective (1996/2000)
She's a Train and She's Dangerous: Women Alone in the 1990s (1994)

the wear of my face

lizz murphy

SPINIFEX

First published by Spinifex Press, 2021

Spinifex Press Pty Ltd
PO Box 5270, North Geelong, VIC 3215, Australia
PO Box 105, Mission Beach, QLD 4852, Australia
women@spinifexpress.com.au
www.spinifexpress.com.au

Edited by Susan Hawthorne and Pauline Hopkins
Cover design by Deb Snibson
Photograph by Camilla Duffy
Typesetting by Helen Christie, Blue Wren Books
Typeset in Albertina
Printed by McPherson's Printing Group

A catalogue record for this
book is available from the
NATIONAL LIBRARY National Library of Australia
OF AUSTRALIA

ISBN: 9781925950342 (paperback)
ISBN: 9781925950359 (ebook)

Supported by

For my family —
I would like to give you the stars

contents

the architecture of pear

with thanks to Margaret

i.

One pear is built by its words the other assembled in paint
lake strokes swirling into wide pear base
They are plain canvas torn duck numbers running in reverse

ii.

To make an edifice of pear
fashion first a coracle
a wherryman a crescent moon

iii.

One pear skips a page
This pear is made from old texts
and the must of books

iv.

If a pear is juicy it is also soft
So is decay
have you thought about that?

v.

Each word about a pear is a word out of it
I assemble it I destroy it the annihilation of pear
The first bite is with a knife

vi.

A pear is an ancient
I hold its history
it rocks in the hull of my hand
I splinter the pear
There is the knife again
but the brush has most command
even more than the tongue
although it does not have taste
It brings me refuge as the sea is breath

vii.

At the moment no one is next to me
just the pear the other is a core

viii.

There is something about pears and newspaper
They read so well together

a woman's work

for Jenni

A woman strips grass   splits cane   dreams the
plant   the loop and stitch   honours with her hands

Her mothers   her aunties   whisper making into
earthfingers   a sieve like a lace leaf   a river fold

A basket carries   child   seed   honey   snares an eel
a scoop nets   echoes   the bend of tree   turn of stone

Pandanus   wickers first light   twines red desert
banded goanna   burnished wood   the purple storm

She dreams tradition   the rising pattern of women
cordyline to songline   mist falling   clouds adrift

goes bush   her country   her body   sedge   rush
waratah   white fig bark   witnesses   emu and hawk

cuts barrga strands   passes into flame   or the willowy
straps of the lawyer cane basket   its fine bicornual sweeps

its generous mouth   dreams wild dog dillybag   whiteant
creekcreature   russetsun   the shape of story   without end

A woman's work   preserve   attain   share new knowledge
for women to make   women to lift the mist   unfurl the blue

A woman works   her ochre map   arid weave   corella wing
sand   fire   water   her open-cut land   speaks

some things are orange

for Merlinda

He is hands and knees on newspaper as though
reading closely a blueprint of the civic centre The crisp
of his dark suit protected his loose shirt stark
a vermilion motif a charcoal tie divide Bottled orange
dye is poured over spreading fingers he examines
the changes of colour his rotating indigo wrist
mellowing light murmuring purple-necked pigeons
a magpie choir jazzing offstage

One shopfront has skewered awning edges and upper
windowsills pigeons no longer roost there only
sycamore leaves pinned up to dry or to mull over later
like all those things we mean to champion but leave
to honest-to-goodness activists

The two men soon depart their desideratum rolled
in an armpit his one tangerine hand out to the left of
him a talking point back at the office

Here is an idea for a sculpture A worse-for-wear
goddess and her fauna decipher the transmuting
seasons She wears an erect collar of silver spike and
bract and a violet-winged headdress Her wrist bones
peacock her skin peeling citrus arteries persimmon
The red carneau nesting in there thinks it's a fable

A woman sits on a nearby bench wrapped in a warm black overcoat burgundy knit beret   She is her own writing bureau Huon Pine pockets and pigeon-holes her lap a drop-leaf   her crossed legs twist-turn cedar

They do not talk

They do not even see each other

There is a forest

This is not the first time I have thought to sculpt Once it happened on a waffled lakebed The poets an arrangement of standing stones unused to space wind   hair dragged about their inscribed throats rimy ears battered by their own cogitations At their backs the rift valley rise the deepening olive of volcanic fold gully sclerophyll leaf   the scurfy stemmed saltbush rinsing the foreshore mallow

stray birds 1–10

after Rabindranath Tagore

i.

I was the stray bird
at your window
we flew

ii.

little vagrants
on the wing
my breath catching
on every arc

iii.

the world was ours
we thought forever
now the oaks are on the turn
my heart breaks open
on your song

iv.

after the rain
birds fall on the drunk grass
still I am drunk on you

v.

your touch slight
a feather
there is laughter
we fly again

vi.
your feathers fall
splinters of the sun
I collect them

vii.
the trees
we planted together
singing above us
birds two by two
their small nests

viii.
a night bird
strikes its delicate bells

ix.
under the dear moon
birds dream
we dream
I dance

x.
love is peace
a flutter in the silence

the wear of my face

for Richard

Graffiti on my right eardrum
It is childhood scarring

Six wild horses
Five stop to stare

The other I hear her say behind
the camera is hiding in the scrub

The beauty of them
and they are dog meat

I think you have to wear your face
he told me it wasn't anything personal

I dreamt of torture I said and I was the
perpetrator   I felt after   like the waking dead

Waiting for the fire to take   I slow-blink
The rims of my eyelids crescents of ice

you can be cruel to a bee

With the open eave of her scarf she catches the tree snags blue winter
Skylight ceiling of criss and cross In the naming of them colours empty
of themselves is this a quote she no longer knows Straight off pavement
licked lyrics you are the outlaw you split dawn shoot footloose tread
threads they cut out his he/art place it on the dead man's chest that's
the show weighed out in small portions organs attuned to a tune There
is the pulse of stars the screech of their last stop her life in another
universe a family shard visiting from one time or another in the same
time Earthing when she is most There are moments when this land
opens fetches her in who knows why it would be so but can you feel it?
The world spins before each crisis she thinks the fog is too grey there
is mass manipulation   the lie is hard as knee caps shattered truth
a curious man children of troubles A baptismal veil of mist stretches
from this sea line to that a functional fantasy a fanciful fiction
a fictional function rising from the ground the ploughman's bones the
storm's surge the cyclical incident the nerve of the tree its stubborn grain
its spicy centre the end of its flower cannonade You can be cruel to a bee
Someone said Radio again that other world seeping through open car
windows cracked back doors passing rooms There they go again

girl in a park

Young girl on the far side cardigan sandshoes
picking up meagre light hands grasping swing-
chains high Her rocking There she is again

Apart

Two older girls walk by that way she leaps up runs
to speak quietly urgently to one returns quickly to
her place on the swing rocks everyone else her age
is inside having tea Her breath is visible She is the
girl who went to court because of what her father
did to her

She never leaves me

how's the weather in binalong

with thanks to Kathleen

The sky in Binalong is clear blue   crystal as
decimated sea El Niño is weakening to neutral
but the fire warning is still on alert temps are
increasing again in spite of autumn we wish rain
would drift our way change our white hills verdant

Elsewhere Praise for heroes in the Brussels blast
warms hearts It was warmish in Lahore when the
Easter bomb went off in that amusement park
security forces continue to collect evidence there
is always a child's shoe

neighbours

i.

A broad half-hearted neighbour his sideways lean into an
elevated garden wall a dead-head pluck here there one foot
swinging indifferently above the ground Formation grasses
and hose reels flourishing roses a lattice of cables the birds
love Prickly pear like thorny mittened hands palettes lolling
around prunings waiting for a lift

ii.

Building remnants like toppled palettes and the ripped backs
of old upholstery sure-footed rescue workers a survivor
slumped in an armchair amidst the rubble or picking over
fallen stone neighbours carrying out the dead a child on a
front step same address no home

strangelands

We are escorted on our way by three blunt-headed silhouettes one above the other and a fourth bringing up the rear After we arrive another parrot is a broad vermilion swoop up to the eves as I look out a magpie is a cat shadow between the bushes

These strangelands where everyone is in and out of their front back and side doors like unremitting cuckoo clocks shrubs pruned steps blown plants watered sluiceways swept bins emptied by mechanical arms brought in two at a time Birds clamour voices drift dogs bark then quiet as the heat rises after midday what strangeness is going on where now

what is he making in there

after Tom Waits

His garage doors open to the wide world his back turned on
the outside world his shoulders rounded over his work world
The buzz and roar world its glow his masked face aglow in
that world what is he doing in there in his world His bin is
bulging His bin is overflowing with stuff plastic stuff what
does he do with all those bottles what does he need those for
What is he creating in there   that old man what business does
he have making things things that glow

preambles

This couple lean and worn in who never leave their home
town have travelled wait not so patiently for the next
stage They'd just be having breakfast around now and
another three hours to go Others flick magazines Young
men poke at the net send texts one up very late stretches
yawns lolls low on one elbow he might as well lie down
sure why not I say

Some stare ahead for a long time you wonder what each
is facing A daughter attempts cheeriness her mother one
foot in a velvety slipper one in dressings as white as
eighty-five year old hair She slumps now in her wheelchair
The vascular team arrives a leggy registrar poses giraffe-like
is excited to be in the theatre gets to watch over shoulders
might get to hitch a stitch or two

another day

with thanks to the Belconnen Arts Centre

The orchestra arrives busy magpies in their black
and whites   chairs and instruments shoved and
strung across the open expanse ducks peeping near
a window savouring their greens before returning
to the lake You take your own leave passing a lone
musician bright as a parrot in a rear corner flipping
music scores her fingers fluttering over each page
You wish you could stay hear her in flight drown out
the thrashing waves fracturing boats someone else's day

exodus

In the dark quilt of witching hour ravens stir black
on midnight blue a full moon lights their way Bomb
tired bullet weary most wait for thistles of daylight
The sun rises on a sea of masks set in grief a blanket
a bundle a child clutched to chests Some with not a
person left in this world

'war zone tours'

I Can Tell You What It's Like

I can tell you what it's like ears and eyes out on stalks neck cricking over one shoulder or another heart in a vice of fear rifles at attention on every corner tanks and jeeps changing the colour of your afternoons people you have known running for their lives work mates afraid to sit near you and maybe you them Family men turned guard and vigilante guns in their pockets women doing normal shopping dropped to the ground a bullet in the back people on a harmless night out in pieces across the pavement I can't start to tell you about the children I can tell you what it's like sitting in your mind-your-own-business living room listening to gunshot getting heavier and closer not knowing whether to go or stay if your street will be cordoned off with barbed wire overturned vehicles the men with guns and should you be kept in or better not Taking your name off the front doorbell so you can't be categorised or bombed out sirens on the increase helicopters low in the sorry sky I can tell you what it's like after you leave and you have begun picking up your own pieces and every week you are watching on the news your country burning watching the news for people you know dead injured evacuated and some days you see them I can't start to tell you what that's like Just stay away from the war zone it's not a sideshow alley there is no step-right-up you have no business there

knots

What knot are you in now? One of your own making? All those animals: worms under- and over-hydrated songless canaries on their backs puppies grown old vets treating and treating You can't keep doing it they see your flaws in the knots you have never had use for A half-hitch? Though you have used the reef knot no prising required the world falls apart of its own avail A child says your house is old you could fix it you say yes I could and carry on levering at life

please leave the door open

with thanks to my family

I lay me down for an afternoon rest listening to thunder
the fan the banter their voices drifting up the hall their
laughter like fine china I remember lying along a sofa
tucked in behind three women The Girls from Work lined
up with their curvy legs round bums their scents: perfume
make-up hairspray nylons Their shoes in pearl blue and
green the misshapen leather toes their bunions and corns
who has the worst my sleep drifting in and out like breathing
the strangeness of my mother laughing she should do
it more often the joy of it Waves of calm another joke
all in good humour waves of delight the smell of more
tea This is what I think it must be like an ending well
tended Someone thoughtful closes the hall door I am not
ready for the silence not yet

bat

for Chris

There is movement on the mantelpiece velvety shadowy
The bat we thought must be in my workroom the room we
closed the door on until night   has landed she stretches
creeps behind candles snuggles into the wall curved ears
scanning It seems bats like poets' houses (not long ago calls
of help from another) She looks dehydrated out of place
gloves cloth a gentle scoop she squirms all the way to the
verandah protests with her tiny voice It is not a bat time of
day it is hot and dazzling but there she goes like some rare
dislocated bird first this way then another lifting lilting to
the tall trees her wing bones drawn white in the sun I taste
the still waters she will drink the next of her life

greyhounds make great pets

with thanks to Sarah

Legs like risen loaves of bread
our heads lolling at the speeding
landscape not taking in the all brown
The odd tree is a thumb swell of khaki
we yearn for an old man kangaroo
an emu a camel a highway robbery
some re-run of history get another
air-con breakdown Someone else's
road trip reminds me of this and the
coach line I will never travel with again
I am now thinking of greyhound racing and
the increasing number of greyhounds out
walking the elegant arc of them
lovingly re-homed instead of you know
what still they have that forlorn mien
A guy on a TV ad confesses to his young wife
I curse: *She is not your mother* So anyway okay
they've got a quick loan
we don't have to hear from them again
and the cat will survive at any cost
Boats scour the water surface white spectators
on open water in their own race and we
on the verge of losing Gonski reform of failing
our children our children failing falling
our children wading neck deep

we tried to tell him

We tried to tell that little red P-plater with the black roof racks that his
black wallet (?) iPad (?) fell off the roof as he veered off in the direction
of Gundagai/Melbourne he was going at a pace but we got level with
him without blocking traffic (well until that car sitting in the right lane
caught up) beeped and beeped and beeped windows down to shout to
him — his aqua T-shirt his fresh haircut pink neck blondish or brownish
— it's lying in the middle of the road before the McDonald's roundabout
Eventually he twigged and pulled over but we couldn't get back into the
left lane to pull over ourselves and our turn-off loomed We imagine he
is still wondering why those bastards were blasting the horn at him or
what is wrong with his vehicle that they saw but he can't If you see a
young guy going pale at his first attempted Visa purchase somewhere
between Yass and Melbourne pass this message on Our failure lies
heavily somewhere in the gut with the monarch butterflies that burst
yellow on our windscreen and the day's fresh egg I dropped in the
chook house when we got home

red

after Patrick Demazeau

It's as if the chairs were here before the trees they
bloom like a poppy understorey A place where absent
ones might sit quietly breathing in forest Red paint
fresh or fading Red is not her mother's colour but
she lays a carnation on each seat One bloom for each
bruise she thinks There are not enough chairs

shock jocks

Rosegold drape cockatoo saw magpie eisteddfod small
bird chitterfest Doors open toilets flush a shock jock
invades you notice a new extension its sky undercoat out
of place This early half hour where everything is alive
settles into crisp stillness

Front doors slamming car engines revving the mass
driveway exit another day each house emptying then
resting on its haunches Behind the peaceful façade a
woman alone with her healing her dread the boozie
smash-mouth nightfall

his

i.

His face ugly with anger framed in the half-lowered car window *You fuckbrat* I had dared to escape from a side street at a roundabout *Read the fuckin rules* I had waited and waited then a pause *Fuckbrat* alongside me now at the traffic lights His speed through the green light The country air torn up

ii.

His vehicle loaded up with grog a good night ahead his many-point turns If only he had waited just a little Me already waiting Waiting to move into a (legal) parking place after delivering to the shopping centre entrance He extracts himself from the tight loading zone (Saturday legal) His screeching face *Why don't you get into the fuckin car park* Not enough drop-off not enough disability parks not enough ramps

iii.

His overly loud *Excuse me!* I am in a traffic jam two rows of shoppers coming down the aisle I want to turn into I take this moment to ask a slowly passing local how she is after surgery (I can multi-skill) My trolley is against the fridge to make way for others I am watching and watching ready to move out of the way That is if I can He wants into the fridge he wants it now His ram of my shopping trolley into my side I turn His face is lumping red yet he is twinkling I think I somehow made his day

zombies

A shop lined with people one bouncing his backside against the
wall at the entrance for something to do another stretched in
a reclining chair having his throat shaved his blonde waves his
alabaster corpselike under fluorescent Under a sari bright floral
leggings around a corner scarlet lips blood-clenched like her eyes
A plump child who keeps reappearing her face as large as her
mother's Everyone is ear-plugged blocking out piped torture
You can find the central checkouts but you can't find the goods
you want A woman in the next seat pops sweets A writer talks of
zombiwords zombilingo corpspeak Bored security guard at the lift
like one of the living dead who is going to steal it a zombi shopper
Escape into sunlight a tall guy broad shoulders squared dusky pink
shirt a pattern short hair longer beard you know neo Ned Kelly
puts someone's bicycle up in a tree I wouldn't know him again

cross my hand

with thanks to David

Under the broadening light of the grapevine lies a door Waiting
moldering waiting for someone to unearth it creak it open
travel downward into its world of bury

I cross my hand over a turned page pick my way around the side
of the pit a root curves under my foot and another like a notion
in a curl of tongue In the back of my mind how we think of the
worst possible scenario to help us cope with reality when it
comes it might be desperate enough anyway

My hand aches from too many words it loses grip My thoughts
tighten and my arm my shoulder He says it's in the last lines the
best ideas come but I can't hold on

> she types
> one finger
> at a time
> her teensy wrists

A helicopter flies low In this other world there is the constant
hum of motors leaf blowers mowers one crashes over sticks
some vehicle reverses at length birds are in and out of the heat

There is a young mother she saunters pushes the pram with
one hand her new babe cradled in the crook of her other arm

> her walk and rock
> walk and rock
> nurturing
> capable

Another thought — the surprise of surprised eyebrows

A small face then a large over there gaunt cheeks eyes dragging she waits for her name to be called

Eyebrows again how they draw them the many ways mostly too high too arced

It skirrs low over the road a wide cape of wing legs like streamers draws back at my approach rises fast I feel these arcs in my own body before it sweeps off in its recast route

          The power
             The grace

like

I write like I am farsighted one eye travelling the white landscape a
centimetre from my face peering around the ink of purple corners
skipping into beaten egg doorways gazing wantonly through domestic
windows spying on tamed strangers I write like the striped suit high-
jinxing with city cars — I am jollification outside the office I write like I
am in live theatre sitting at a table-for-one and an extremely large dinner
plate perched at the entrance of a tepid evening my feet practically on
the pavement milling pedestrians my extras [Lights! Action!] A fan
stirring A breeze my hair tussling   Electric blue moonfish in the dark
lapping water I write like I am the extra trying not to trip up the stars
or the stairs I write like I have been de-veined like a green tiger prawn
to be tossed in a hot pan I inhale the garlic write like I am the main
course I write like a disruption like a wounded eagle like a rent dream
a tangled sheet I write like the homeless sign on a cardboard tear like
somewhere in the world a book has fallen open like the young man
who cries in the wind like the animal on the roof like demand like a
ruffian like self-delight like the fading horizon the fruiting moon the
nest-raiding currawong the bird caught in the net like a sleeve of tension
like a frosted pane like antithesis like a siren like Terpsichore I try to
dodge similes have more success with fullstops.

i suffer not the work of fern

I suffer not the work of fern creeper forest to reach the coast with its faraway ocean stare its mountain scalloped blue its ponytailed jogger population scoring paths across green its youth hanging out not on the beaches but around nightclubs and in late evening convenience stores Long and blonde built for the gym in bananayellow clingwrap slinging legs over the stranger's Harley-Davidson cool way to meet the ownerguys rapidly reappearing the girls' smartphones snapping up eyecandy Or brown and slight flicking lights at their cigarettes high pitched bright trinket voices black skirts like resistive exercise bands around cherry-size bottoms and I should speak once upon a time An orange and white skullface takes admission across the road I fish for the last of ample prawns in my windowseat laksa Chopsticks point me at memories where I once strolled this humid place familiar but strange in its changes I know any minute now something may happen in the way of the past chancing on the present a re-visitation an invisible hoik from the rear a nudging line or a mutter from the future   premonitions my forte My chary eye over my shoulder my ready hand behind an ear

this is what we do

Watching expert diners I realize I hold my chopsticks too
low down I had supposed I used them quite well shown
how by my husband's regular taxi fare Young woman
brought home to meet me (He talked about me a lot)
Japanese-Chinese heritage She could speak four
languages design a dress draw the pattern cut it out sew
it up all in just two hours *This is what we do* she said
simply In another café a Chinese man battles to use a fork
Scoops at each pea one by one Loses each pea one by one

lines

She hated her thyroid scar Like a cut throat she said But it
wasn't that bad the knife held steady an arc of fine silk
thread scattered seed pearls The third pregnancy she
didn't want how she must have felt hovering on the brink
of those stairs That third daughter unaware The broken
smile on the Egyptian princess her dried form small as a
child's the state of her bandages A luminous white line
stretching around a bend spaced 'cat's eyes' glinting like the
suture marks on a thyroid surgical scar

all i could see

All I could see simple directions raucous music their labels
faded full glasses groaning and the small craft we've gone
outside It drifted off when the moon flooded the oil lamps
burned I saw her signing shadows mournfully wearing
only the long dress a crept smile the smell of scorching
wood the thin sickle sigh of relief some type of old Gaelic
They are water creatures fit into a bigger pattern

right of way

With thanks to Glenyse, Janene, Moyra

A grey sunless building its bones arthritic but on that day in that top window a goddess child's face Architecture rattles me as much as ancient dresses in a museum or an empty iron cot This is a street in Launceston Thought you'd like the architecture and the park gates I liked the man on the corner shuffling his glasses back into place and the bare branches reaching like wrought iron for the steeple nosing into the sky How many plastic bags do you think a whale's stomachs can hold? I could have felt alone driving through the desert but each tussock spoke to me and once in a while a road sign said yes you are still going the right way

PS Of course the wind turbines usually wave

bag

The smell and texture of a small plain loaf (unsliced) when loaves (sliced) were in greaseproof wrappers when cellophane wraps arrived with an orange sun on the side (Sunblest) how you could see its black crust (crunchy) through the paper Now a loaf comes in a plastic bread bag sealed with a plastic bread bag clip (foreign body) frequently ingested by young children and edentulous adults Luckily I still have my teeth (just) As the daughter of a shoe mender who held his tacks inside his bottom lip one always primed for action between his teeth I hold bunches of small nails or thumbtacks in my mouth any time I have a hammer in my hand my teeth on duty as guard rail (but still — don't breathe in) Billions of bread bag clips are produced each year landfill mountains are made from them we are encouraged to upcycle (guitar picks book marks key and cable identifiers jewellery a very very large collage)

(more ducks)

On another road there are many ducks crossing they
slow us down to a crawl A car in the righthand lane
beep-beeps One duck *leaps* flashes legs and silver
under-wings like that elderly man sauntering in the
middle of the street a horn blast and him vaulting into
the air his silver comb-over lurching forward without
him In the bakery the Chinese woman wishes me
Happy Australia Day her beautiful mouth smiling off
her face as she sings the price of my lunch

happy days

Foxy happiness written all over his triangle face
chocolate in the early light pacing his boundaries
up first thing to watch the commuter parade his young
pipe cleaner twist of body and tail his lankiness his
tongue hanging pink Him and his kind wrecking the
gorge its fragile grasses its endangered bird species
Even the town chickens are at risk

felt

Arms face folded in determination or boredom she stares intently at his diminishing cheesecake feigning interest There is some autocue that permits another couple to start in on their apple and cinnamon muffins They slice and butter The cut side like beige felt

Felt: *once used as a filter*

A sales assistant carries an elderly customer's plant selection The small talk is that neverending story of weather whether it will rain or not Her husband was a pilot and he used to say … Damn it I have stuck my head in the back of my car What would he know from up there in his old cockpit

Filter: *a piece of felt*

Three women Two demanding One quiet One mother trying to outdo one gregarious daughter The other mostly silent They leave at last: the mother the gregarious daughter the quiet daughter The quiet daughter's step is quiet as felt The others march stride strut on well-heeled clamour

No filter

dark space

The Travelling Insurance Man is home Shirt stainstriped
Interchangeable starched collar blindingly white His
adolescent daughter blinks awkwardly the unexpected
visitor shifting things causing her to notice he is wearing
his week's menu He is relaxed and pleasant enough in his
armchair enjoys a new child audience for his opinions
On another day his wife will put her head in the gas oven
The daughter will come home in time to drag her out will
be afraid to leave her alone ever again These glimpses are
dark space between the stars they silence us We never
mention this again

scintillate

GPS got you lost? Found yourself back in that same car park? Caught on a rural dirt road with no way to turn your motorhome around? There may be a severe space weather event above you Instabilities most serious after sunset your GPS may 'scintillate' The sun is our closest star just average a middle-aged dwarf past its prime but still a few billion years to go and fierce is its heat Its domains: interior surface atmospheres inner corona outer corona Did someone say *Corona?* There are days during Coronavirus when everything seems as normal as it ever is There are days when you wonder if the sun will rise again still spherical still orange Or will it be blue with purple protrusions red spikes embellished colour as feared as the pathogen itself

forecast

… and it occurs when new stars form at a high rate inside/Add a handful of blooms/pretty those collisions of temper/little killers/ under the dark/crying to heaven/as the earth reeled beneath/stood aghast …

Rows of clouds ahead like a great feather and down doona how cold it looked and still my surprise when I drove into the sudden chill I am no weather forecaster *could have blocked out comets in earth-crossing orbits.*

Ceres the dwarf planet orbited by the spacecraft *Dawn* Ceres the Roman goddess of the growth of food plants agriculture and grain Ceres the Goddess of Bread where was she in The Famine Ceres the goddess a poet sent to hell *Dawn* is retired now Still orbiting Uncontrolled

unlike a black cat

View the Goldilocks Variable
  through the nebula velocity

Have you thought about space weather?
Very low solar activity is expected today
Geomagnetic activity mostly: Quiet

Your hands
turn clay
drive out evil
cure diseases

unlike a black cat
which brings bad luck
though some say not

That melon moon
We dried those seeds in saucers by the fire
strung them into lengths the needle crackling
through papery husk patience pricked
as much as our small fingers

catchcry

'Our children are our future'
That catchcry bandied about
so often
Often
so empty

'Our children are our future'
Those little legs pedalling that bike
She will want to pedal time
backwards

'Our children are our future'
everyone would say
and now our children say
they have no future

They say
we have stolen it
we destroyed it
we failed it

They say
we are failing them
They say
'How dare you!'

Every day
the tampering with the sacred
the fragmenting of rock
thousands of feet
walking
climbing
scarring

takings

The old clock, which stood in the hall

I have one in my kitchen No honey characterless pedestrian
like something you would find in a train station In the waiting
room a passenger waiting Her *tickings seemed to vibrate* Worry
through her every nerve Checks her tickets checks her watch checks
the pedestrian clock on the pedestrian wall Makes small talk
in the waiting room Waits on the edge of her nerves

at last told the hour

Mid-sentence
a tall boy stands
bares his calf
The glimpse of ink
his non-stop excitement
So much news
so much to plan
so much
so important

A basic recipe urn of blood a dress stained crimson
red mushrooms through fabric

They gouge excavate take and take
they own them now
have them in the scoop of their hands
They rope them in with the short-term offer
Jobs for the strugglers
Jobs for the so-called future
The hold they have
There is no reparation

Countries suffer
let them go

threats

Take for example/bones of malleefowl

Extinct giants in the sediment layers Malleefowl
ancient fossilised Today's malleefowl vulnerable
threatened extinct Depending on the area you live
in Highly sensitive to the grazing of sheep fire
fragmentation Ground-dwelling but they can
fly fly into the violet into the blue

How much we worry about our own anatomy
how it functions how it malfunctions A gentleman
discreetly sweeps his hand across his denim front
Everything in situ

A llama stands against the wind one eye closed the
other lee-side ears arching inward a collar of
wool ringing its neck Llamas spit when they feel
threatened they spit to deter predators That
would work Llamas also hum

locks

How many teeth does a healthy sheep have in the top of its mouth?|
The wildly tender voice said again

Note that unpalatable spiky style that spread coming
up short The magpie lifts arcs Feet poised as if already
locking on to that fine branch just above the road's
shoulder A bicycle braced on top of the car in front
suddenly drops at a right angle to the roof How the
driver must've jolted He arcs into the first side street to
lock everything back into place Someone has turned
their back   a wave rises like a great fist

cracks

He seemed very breezy and fit

It's snowing plastic in the Arctic Microplastics in sea-ice Microplastics in seabirds The Northern fulmar a plastics magnet This is the Ice-Edge There are cracks and meltwater pools the shrinking glint of glacier The scientist drills into 'fast ice'

The animal turns its rear to that sullen rain no scarlet shelter in a city where it always rains and is often windy Inside-out umbrellas a common turn spokes racing through fabric whipped out of the owners' hands swept across town plunged into some high privet *She steps out of the leafy* If you can't unworry try the worry beads around her neck *I think that is utterly*

and, look —
anxious —

the black dog gets first prize again
as *the red dwarf star/sketches by*
becomes swarf

out upon the darkness
the boats are launching again

prey

Faint winged you feel your body mirror
the quirk of another that particular
crook of hip that midriff tuck as she
reaches Her downward glance

WARNING

TEAR GAS

SMOKE

throat seemed to close as if he we
were prey a tiger circling
gifted hunter draws his claws

penalty

i.

The child settled now her mother's arm around her the
long wait Up again The slight of her On her toes with
expectancy Those weird and wonderful creatures
perched like birds on a branch the coffee line on stools
one picks at her phone like a parrot nibbling a seed her
strong neck her S-curved ear Standing two steps back
from the jeweller's window she dreams of an emerald
ring hands loosely passively by her side feet planted What
is in her mind Is she working up to buying it for herself or
to throwing a smash-and-grab through the plate glass

ii.

That head of hers Its ultramarine Rose madder Its
vermilion eye A fine line on a wall a small moth on one
side of it the smudge of gilt wing powder on the other
Face patchy in the blue serge moonlight *She freed herself
wildly, lined against the sky*. *I may breed* She picks up a leaf
it is blood in her hand but what a sublime shape She rises
above his scrambled mind Writing her greeting card she
keeps her cheerful mood in the face of his foul Penalty for
failure Notices will continue carry the same weight in the
brewing political wreckage Please do close your knees I
can see your thighs roll right up to the top

rips

She wings through the aerosphere casts mauve
shadows cuts through ice thaws frost Leaves crinkle
become brittle She is a star performer thinks she is
a smash In a waiting room a woman's hair grows
long her plait tentacles her past a sealed room her
daughter a rent of silk by her side

What of this plastic he says with his plucked turkey
head tilting upward The old white woman of the
night hoots low and long Her sigh fans the ocean
creates a rip tide a wave of polymer sweeps deep

brown goshawk

Accipiter fasciatus

I am beguiled by the yellow
of your eye the bright pierce of it

You skirring overhead
wrists pushed forward

Me looking up
into the blue squint

You more interested in luckless burrowings
at my feet than in my hollowing thoughts

in the mottled unwelcome sparrow or the
black and white flash of the strenuous magpie

Your frowning steel grey smudges into rufous
the colour of   turned earth   or dried blood

Menace clips at my elbow
fear loops deep in my belly

It's last
wretched beak clap

Your strike
that thud

My shudder
I am plucked half bare

mourning

The currawong mourns On the hospital
road In my dreams My arms around her
wide black shoulders my condolences her
apprehension

Ahead skirt snagged on her waistband
dear old thighs backs of knees miniature
lilac waterscapes long life long day

conundrums

I am waiting in the waiting room with Mary Oliver celebrating
nature Leaving I am greeted by slashing sunlight and a
magpie chorister We are both happy to see blue after deluge
after deluge At lunch the breaking news is terrorism we will
check our friends' itinerary when we get home In the car park
a gentleman scrummaging in the pocket of his thoroughly
worn okay-for-around-the-yard tracksuit pants inadvertently
pulls them out of the leather belt hitching them up We leave
him with his half-mast conundrum without quite enough
hands with the world raising its flags

the refuge of art

with thanks to Marianne

Here I am again in a gallery Afloat in the wide space in the white The white walls the light the images on the white walls the light the space the white on white the colour the contrast the tint the tone the lack of tone the line the straight line the curved line the arc the line arcing into me Out there it is chaos the corridors the fluorescent lights the buzzers the beeps the blips the screens the drips The doctors who haven't arrived yet the doctors you have just missed the charts the blue scrubs the stethoscopes the pills the lack of pills the forms The nurses coming the nurses going changing shift You go over it all again You take a little time out Here you are again in a gallery afloat

points

Draw heartbreak she said and lines cracked the page Make it
a piano and the pencil shaped keys legs a black ebony lid and
a small man in a hat standing on top of it like he had claimed
ground someone's homeland Add a pony she said and the rough
of a head with fly-twitching ears emerged and a brawny backside
like a quarter horse's his legs not unlike the piano's The piano
needs feet she said and they were like bad hands or her inbred
Silkie hen's feet The man seemed to be pronouncing his finger
pointed the type who would want to plant a flag so she gave him
one she also gave him three stars they had points this doesn't

signals

with thanks to Peter

At the lake a seagull's iris is a minute tub of white shoe polish
he waits patiently for the treat that does not come *Please do
not feed the birds in public places* I catch these snippets on the car
radio *makes them aggressive* A crowd gathers it's like some silent
command has been given one of the newcomers humps the
back of his neck as if about to disgorge squawks loudly then tail
up stretches his neck forward extends his throat heaves out his
longcall his chokingcall *I should be first in the queue* he repeats and
repeats Another looks left to right and around about as if to ask:
*What did he say? Does anyone know what's going on here? What is it I
am supposed to be doing?* I relate Drive away

At the T-section a new sign says: *We are signalizing this intersection*
I imagine flag semaphore lucky that some Girl Guides and
Boy Scouts still practise it A 'Seagull intersection' is a three-
way road thing How often havè I driven on a 'seagull's wing'
without realizing I'd taken flight? We drive through the green
of recent rain scatters the colour leaching the closer we are to
home At least the smoke haze has left all of us Turning on to
Burley Griffin Drive an artist (I recognize him) strides casually
across the road you can see he has done this a thousand times
Phone in hand a birl about Biscuit slopes flanking both sides
then phone to ear He has located a signal

first things first

with thanks to Heather and Hilary

He bows to the mild of morning stoops before
the dark of zucchini the blush of tomato a tight-
headed cabbage the crochet texture of silverbeet
his small congregation of sheep waiting patiently
by the gate These early rituals she has swept
the paths the clothes already blowing swaying
on the line a sunrise rinse

wheelbarrow

after William Carlos Williams

The green wheelbarrow is secondhand has a rusted patina
one leg secured by wire spills its contents if you fill it
recklessly is as essential as any red wheelbarrow So much
depends upon it too

At the end of its life the green wheelbarrow replete with
fertile soil and foliage spill will be put to rest in a garden bed
Even now it reminds her of bare mattress histories Mission
children renamed 'Daisy 1' 'Daisy 5' 'Daisy 14' 'Wheelbarrow'

hedge

with thanks to Deborah and Asha

'You look like you've been dragged through a hedge backwards!' I catch
myself in a mirror a tumbledaboutwindfalllookwhatthewindblewin
never a comb on me poke at some strands vain attempt to put things
in place I've been dragged through that hedge backwards I say to myself
Now I am the hedge Not privet Not that dusty cobwebby caterpillar-
ridden hedge of childhood not that air-choking allergen of the suburbs
I'm going for an Irish native Let's try hawthorn its branches weighted
with white blossom and later startlingly orange berries irresistible to
blackbird with its bright beak the cyanide seed no hindrance to song
What about some hazel and buckthorn Throw in a wild rose see how
they interthread Or a wildlife fruiting hedge The birds are already here
I am hedge they build their nest

She calls me Big Tree Woman I am taken aback I'm not sure I deserve
this yet I feel my canopy grow soar spread Lime and crimson shoots a
crowd of them singing Singing breath into being My feet take root bind
into earth break through dry reach water My roots share moisture with
earth and other trees I am community My hair is nest Chicks sheeny
black sing out to their mother There she is sailing so close I feel the air
move I know her She who leaves her calling cards on the screen door
A small contour feather raincloud grey A fulsome gum leaf musk pink
A spotted semiplume from a passing guineafowl I see other women as
Tree Women Women of age or coming of age the marks on their once
smooth bark The curves and crevices Life ingrained Who needs tattoos

who's been eating the moon

for Bill

The moon is still up burning the candle at both ends one edge eaten out by blue We drive into grey Here the air has reached dew point is devouring the moon Not much road left either

To the rear feeding grey and pink flocks move as one The occasional reaching wing a stretch a private joke a pale rose head rising A sudden calling and they lift shoulder to shoulder flap out a circle settle again A momentary threat or false alarm

Our own galah wing clipped free to wander eyeing off the other birds laboriously walks up the six-foot fence down the other side across the top paddock up the four-foot boundary fence down the net and barbed wire several metres to the edge of the large assembly No one utters a word He spends the morning with them His gruelling return journey his dodder his large grey feet Every day we watch for his safe homecoming In spring he rediscovers flight

We can't know if he is gone from our lives if he calls out *G'day* and *Mum* over someone else's home or if each season he nests here has offspring in the nearby creche tree alive with gurgling fledglings Perhaps he flies overhead just once in a while checking out how mature our eucalypts are now as glad as we are that some of our tree plantings survived those droughts

back to basics

I lost something from back then the newness the play the freefall
the curious landings the willingness a naivety Bared dreams
dissected like birds on the dinner table their folded wings crisp
the tips charred black like nibs dipped don't say ink don't use the
pen-and-ink simile it is too common Though alluring with its
blueblack on silver black on white the anticipation of line and
now it too an oddity and keyboards don't ring of metaphor What
can you dip them in They are for smearing or drizzling yes drizzle
and drip notions meanings gists Where is this going Back to basics
We were on a beach but only in my imagination now we are
inlanders blown dry husked of bark freshly tinted veneer waiting
for another bucketing The next scorching

old spice

with thanks to Wayne and the Liberty Salon

He was two rows away but I could smell the iron on that man's shirt Fine white threads permeated with uncommon domesticity I connect with the back of fathers' necks clean shaven after a weekly visit to the barber his lean fingers flitting the comb the scissors hovering   waspish Red leather stained timber Bronze studded old quality Old Spice yes some still use it Snipping and clipping tingle and sting and the squat brush flicking around all those ears You sitting on the long settle bench waiting your turn and studying napes how they fold over a collar or in on themselves incised with the years   The idea of it

lost property

A blackhead the size of a fastener out of his sight You'd like to tell
him but what could he do he lived alone his top drawer full of
notes Interest is what you get on money in the bank if you have
any or what the bank takes if like most of us you have borrowed
sums It's what you hope people will show in your work even if you
say otherwise *Fuck I'm busted!* is what you say if you are an
elderly woman who barely made it up the steps to go to that
funeral All minds on the dead and no one else Not even those
almost there find your own way Kites Found tangled around
telegraph wires sometimes there is a pair of sandshoes no lost
property box for them The best weather for flying kites Windy
obviously but what about today would the kite rise above this
bluster or be nosedriven into the ground like some plan of yours
Birds well you may laugh

who will bury the pensioners

Old people beaten up for their cash you wonder how they could have any on pensions but that generation survived the Depression they're used to looking after the pennies and the pounds that looked after themselves they bury under the mattress or at the back of the shelves baiting wanton thieves because the government will slash their payments if their shavings show any savings But who else will bury them?

the power of prayer

His cab parked kerbside
brown sock soles shining
he kneels and bows his silken
prayer rug the hush of him
This taxi rank worshipping place
the sycamore's embroidered bark
its shimmering lime canopy

what does it take to make white

And overnight it has snowed the landscape coated white
Only rusted fenceposts and occasional rock mottles the
white paddocks

What does it take to make white The difference between
the sound of rain and the sound of snow thawing A magpie
venturing out by herself her cold feet Driving on roads
melting back to black churned with ice the earth edging up
again vivid green etchings under tree shelter

bleached

Just a week ago the land was a wrung out cloth streaked
gold through olive damp This week it is a bleached sheet
heads of wheaten grass shimmering champagne and
silver with each breeze I have only just left the ghost of
winter behind Everything is opposite

> guitar shaped leaf
> birdraised wing
> downy underside
> second cast shadow
> ghosting winter

prayer: quick & dirty

i.

Listen quick and dirty eight orange stars a vest like a raffle ticket
a limited palette white stir of wind unsettled soils the knowledge of
stone ▾ Her lung a Latin cavity a delta She wears her wonder like a
bonnet love slung over one shoulder walks with orchids hedges
her bets on the green of leaves cradles nests and sunsets One eye
carving heaven out of earth ▾ His raven eye fitly set wounds Your
takeaway face that glass palace a dove-wash of milk a fluttering
mouth prayerful hands like clacking geese ▾ Listen to him now him
and his raspberry insult cobbles burled by the currents smooth grey
pigeons your palm against him the death of him If you peel back
the pages you will see her porcelain skin is broken china and she is
bone lazy it shows between her eyes and in that torn yattering lip She
tweezes the brow above her mind's eye selects a curly moment from
our prejudices borrows a hard hat a canary going down a mine or a
hanging garden ▾ Between one body of interest and another there is
outrage or razor wire If you had the power to revoke any moment
which hour would it be the one when wild seas forced that ketch
aground or when she handled the bullet before loading the gun meet
your maker ▾ He is an oracle with two daughters one makes butter
the other gives blood in a landscape crushed to coal a black slide their
slippers a queue of teeth Who has the winning number what colour is
the voucher why is a fox terrier loose in a field of begging ▾ Don't be
shy you sweet me remember to talk dirty to me your arms a sweeping
bird the contours of the land your fingers parting the way Count the
haters endure the scornful tenderize the meek Salvation Rafty water
and sheltered night can't budge this planet She said alas yes this is the
wicked nation this is the hell bent save me save me

ii.

Clay vessels essays of truth we all believe drink tea arrange
posies Wasps build them in keyholes on walls suspend them
thimble-size from beams The fairy-martin lays her eggs in mud
bottles distinguishes the character of her young   like some small
miracle Yesterday's journey an arc of stiletto red under the monotone
of stricken evening Sin familiar and corrugated common as
corduroy the old Singer up on its brawny legs humming Its running
stitch its rapid tacking chronicles this place ▾ The city arrives at the
bus stop and is whisked away again Buses are frequent The woman
with the whopping pink tote bag whisk Now an office worker her
skirt in layers whisk and the overseas student the saint of learning
also the saint of beekeeping whisk The wild shopper multiple store
bags around capsizing knees confession ahead whisk They leave
impressions bereft as votive candles ▾ What is it about devotion The
cheap price of intention the opportunity to escape life this life an
afterlife whisk We are 30,000 feet in the air beneath is reduced to
ceramic mosaic toll roads mountain trails no more than bathroom
grouting the desert freckled hide We hope this trip speaks wish for
the outlandish expect the ordinary course of things observe the small
child her shell-pink complexion her tapestry blue iris her breath an
offering ▾ Will our last supper be better than airplane food whisk Not
much time for a whole life-before-my-eyes or please-god-I've-changed-
my-mind-let-me-in That pelican weekend our new camera that one
time I neglected to ask permission that lunging shuttered second Yes
there was a fabled swan but the pelican yes her legendary bleeding
breast feathering the air so close to my face I had to avert my eyes
as if in prayer

arrivals

We arrive open windows let in cooling air
fragments of loud conversation We ourselves
are talking to Ireland all the family is there for
Christmas (except us) We are talking loud
(because it is far away) I remember the
neighbours again (we are not used to that)
Tonight it is us reverberating across the
narrow street over the fences into the night
No dogs have stirred That's a good thing

bees

with thanks to beekeeping friends

i.

Male bees die after mating
If you are a boy bee stay a virgin

ii.

A bee stung me on the tongue I was in the pram at the
front door with an iced bun My mother saw me just in time
See me trying to get the sting out she said

iii.

A bee makes a twelfth of a teaspoon of honey in its lifetime
She licks every last drop from the bottom of every jar
Her long honeybee tongue

iv.

She asks her beekeeper husband to catch a bee
sting her arthritic joint swears by the cure

v.

The Bee Man wanted to put hives in our violet paddock
We said no A heap of bee boxes appeared just over our fence
Our neighbour got free honey No one got stung

vi.

She has taken up beekeeping Her pantry lined with jars of deep gold
I brought one home today A gift that makes me hum

vii.

A worker bee may visit 2000 flowers in a day
Plant more flowers so they don't have to commute

viii.

If you hear a loud humming from your beehives it is just the workers
fanning the queen with their wings It's summer what do you expect

diapause

An amber striped curve with shriekingback legs
is blown on to my windscreen and there are so few
of you Another bee buzzes around a window
Flyspray too conveniently at hand I squirt Mistaken
identity the blowflies awakened with the warmth
I have often wondered if flies hibernate Not so
Undergo diapause Like the more permanent state
of insect parliamentarians

summer

Summer paddocks ski-slope smooth Sheep dark
as spat up boulders Christmas tinsel around the
pole someone crashed headlong into Season of
Sadness Merry Trinkets Frown on a baby too
young to know frowning Daddy please shade
his eyes Red hot chilli peppers and the
earthquake she felt face down in the green river
She is comfortable in her big ass cool-as-
cucumbers steps lightly around *what you want
me to be* A loud voice looping through the
crowds a chimp in a food hall jingle A swarming
insect hum That screeching bird Post-Xmas Sale
wresting every last dollar Happy Poor Year

'you don't pay for any fancy overheads'

i.

There are a dozen maybe more mainly men spreading through
our small store selecting multiple items or scooping up armfuls
ignoring the young sales assistants (Thursday night casuals) They
stream to the three checkouts pile merchandise on to the
counters More streaming in behind them the girls going as fast
as they can on the cash registers They are about to wrap and the
'customers' walk off again and again A protest Stay calm I say
come on to help fold and bag then return the consistently
rejected goods the girls rapidly cancelling the sales on the tills
I go into my super-sweet the-customer-is-always-right-can't-
thank-you-enough mode It's the Union I don't know what has
happened but this store is a target our busy late night 'no fancy
overheads' shopping is a target the kids are the fallout They are
stressed bewildered almost fainting Pick on someone your own
size Never did find out what Best & Less had done Unless it was
after that staff cut Last employed first to go a strong unionist
That wasn't the kids' fault

ii.

A beige man visits the family-size factory speaks to each worker
heads for me I'm new More or less my first job Do I want to join
the Union? 'The Union?' No such talk in my house I ask at home
anyway Oh yes you should always join your Union I'm given the
money It still isn't talked about

iii.

Another new job another beige man In my moment of reflection (probably remembering the first time) a senior co-worker approaches chin and shoulder first says other staff won't want to work with someone who isn't a union member I'm put in my place I was going to join anyway

protests

with thanks to all those brazen hussies

Women's Liberation protests on the news Black-and-white
blur Grainy faces in the camera Shouting mouths

EQUAL PAY
EQUAL EDUCATION
EQUAL RIGHTS

One woman two young girls two little boys in a frozen state —
do not go out of the house do not say a word — watch those
free women free to shout to call it out — sit still do not sigh
audibly do not give an opinion do not roll your eyes keep your
eyes on the TV The fuckin TV always on filling the deadly void

***

How did you know about Women's Liberation? It's agreed it
was in the air And also on TV in the news all over the news
Those women Those girls Their strike for freedom

nobody's child

with thanks to Robert

It's a fraying wind that takes her back into
that box where they needle cut slam with
acidic words and hands No locks on doors
or leaf-curtained windows but no out it
wasn't worth her life to leave

                    to stay

                        to leave

kids half price

crossing

overcrowded   not   looking good

50   squeezed in

half a foot of water   mounting alarm

doomed

"For God's sake,

stop moving!"

rippling waves,

they all pray.   our final destiny,"

kids half price,

too many times   sinking

engine   no   drifting

water still coming in?"

rising

tangle of legs.

bale out

capsizes,

container lorries

suffocation

syria's children

after Magnum Wennman

i.

These children
bare ankled
dusty kneed
belly down
on flock
They stare
You see
they have died
over and over

ii.

A mock mattress a sheet her pink
striped socks like scattered litter
the forest floor the closed border
                    her freezing body her sleep

iii.

He slumps into
his backpack
this bleak pillow
Asphalt grates
small kneecaps
elbows
Bombs grate
footworn dreams

iv.
She sleeps with her eyes open and
bright as the stars though her sky
is overcast a cloud-grey coat pulled
up to her bonny nose

v.
The quiet of an infant
who understands nothing
of flight or teargas or why
he sleeps under just a jacket

vi.
You would know him by his flaxen hair
the flatness of his ear the number on his jeans
pocket otherwise he is like so many children of this
war lying like a disposed-of small body in some
refugee wilderness feet aching memories
exploding sanctuary sliding

vii.
He is a Kouros statue lain to rest in the town
square his elongated face young lips
long narrow feet gathered in on his stone bed
How can he sleep   how can he ever sleep

viii.

One million children are fleeing

Some languish on the roadside but she
has landed a hospital bed and she sleeps and sleeps
the flush of acute illness on her infant cheeks

One million children are fleeing

ix.

She covers her face
with her headscarf
and one beautiful hand
Her sleeping infant
limp-limbed across her lap
Her grief as unshakeable
as the slammed iron gate

blood moon

You go black like a lid closing curtains drawing on
a show the end of a film Nothing stirs or changes
for a time then a spark and your flickering edge It
happens just as I am about to leave it's like the
credits have begun to roll and I am compelled to
stay to read all those names

Out here I could honour them aloud privately
ceremoniously in the pleasant chill under silent
leaves all those people who have offered a kindly
word some small praise a plaudit kept some
thready person tacked together one more day

There is one more flare a wreathing light then the
leaden cloud veils you charcoal I go inside trusting
in tomorrow

endnotes

Page 1
I am very grateful to Margaret Shepherd of Crookwell NSW for one of the first inspirations for *The Architecture of Pear* — a small painting/collage which I loved, on show in the Goulburn Art Gallery shop.

Page 3
A Woman's Work was written for the opening of Jenni Kemarre Martiniello's exhibition *Glass Weave* Belconnen Art Centre, 2012, after a spellbinding visit to the Canberra Glassworks to watch Jenni at work and to visit her studio there.

Page 4
The lake scene in *Some Things are Orange* was inspired by a fascinating poetry workshop facilitated by Merlinda Bobis at Lake George/Weereewa NSW. Thank you also to dancer Elizabeth Cameron Dalman who hosted the weekend at her Mirramu Creative Arts Centre.

Page 6
Stray Birds 1–10 is after Rabindranath Tagore's poem of the same title.

Page 8
I am forever grateful to dear Richard Conrick (RIP) and cracker sister-out-of-law Elena Garcia, for the collision of conversations which resulted in the poem *The Wear of My Face*.

Page 11
How's the weather in Binalong? was written in response to a poetic personal message from Kathleen McCracken in Ireland.

Page 12

Neighbours (i) and many other suburban poems are set in the District of Belconnen, ACT, with thanks to our son Brendan and his beloved wife Helen.

Page 14

What Is He Making in There? is after the Tom Waits song *What's He Building?* on the album *Mule Variations* (ANTI-1999).

Page 18

War Zone Tours was written in response to the article 'Russian travel company wants to sell tours to the front line of Syrian civil war' published at news.com.au, January 2016. <http://www.news.com.au/travel/world-travel/middle-east/russian-travel-company-wants-to-sell-tours-to-the-front-line-of-syrian-civil-war/news-story/f68110a7e1a10c7e34a5837896afe83e>

Page 22

Greyhounds make Great Pets — the Gonksi report was a landmark review of school funding announced by the Rudd/Gillard government in 2010, which aimed to address a growing gap between high and low performing students. At the time Australia had one of the biggest gaps among developed countries. In 2013 the Liberal government announced it would reverse Labor's Gonski-based school funding model, only keeping it for 2014 its first year of implementation. In 2021 educational equity is still declining. For more information on the Gonski report try:

The Conversation 'What is a Gonski anyway?' by Bronwyn Hinz, 20 April, 2013 9.07am AEST. <https://theconversation.com/explainer-what-is-a-gonski-anyway-13599>

The Guardian 'Tony Abbott defends Gonski reversal, saying election pledge was misheard' by Daniel Hurst. 1 December 2013. <https://www.theguardian.com/world/2013/dec/01/abbott-defends-gonski-reversal-misunderstood-promise>

For an update you might like to visit the Gonski Institute for Education, UNSW Sydney: 'Structural failure: Why Australia keeps falling short of its educational goals.' Accessed April 25, 2021. <https://www.gie. unsw.edu.au/structural-failure-why-australia-keeps-falling-short-its-educational-goals>

Page 24
Red is a response to an installation titled *The Four Seasons of Vivaldi* by Patrick Demazeau (2001).

Page 27
Zombies includes a fragment remembered from an interview with Louise Katz titled 'Words Stripped of Meaning: A Guide to Linguistic Spam' on *The Conversation* ABC Radio National, August 5, 2016. You might also like to read 'Zombie Words are Coming for your Brains' by Jen Doll in The Atlantic. July 25, 2012. <https://www.theatlantic.com/culture/archive/2012/07/zombie-words-are-coming-your-brains/325522/>

Page 35
Right of Way was sparked by Irish poet Moyra Donaldson's touching poem *Postcard from the Island of Lizards* in *Beneath the Ice* (Lagan Press 2001); also inspired by an arresting photo of the Living Goddess Kumari in Kathmandu by Glenyse Ings (1985) and a photo I took in Launceston (2014).

Pages 43–53
The poems *Forecast* through to *Penalty* incorporate excerpts from *Typewriter Used by a Newspaper's Office* one of my artist books, which is compiled from fragments of found text and image, from magazines, science journals and old books.

Sources include:
Dawn (spacecraft) — Wikipedia. <https://en.m.wikipedia.org>
Marie Claire June 2009

Racing Pace by Olive Wadsley, Cassell & Company Ltd, London, Toronto, Melbourne and Sydney c.1930
Science Illustrated Australian Edition #52

In addition:
The poem *The Making of an Irish Goddess* by acclaimed Irish poet Eavan Boland (RIP) begins with Ceres going to hell (see *Forecast* page 43); *Unlike a Black Cat* (page 44) also includes information from the Bureau of Meteorology; *Catchcry* (page 45) — *How dare you!* was said by 16 year old Greta Thunberg, dynamic Swedish climate activist, to world leaders at the United Nations Climate Summit in New York, 23 September 2019. Greta's full speech can be viewed at <https://www.youtube.com/watch?v=KAJsdgTPJpU> The Uluru Statement from the Heart may also be of interest. See <https://ulurustatement.org/the-statement>

Page 59
The Refuge of Art gelled after a stimulating conversation with US poet Marianne Boruch about art as solace (her word) or refuge (my word), during her 2019 visit to Canberra on a Fulbright Scholarshop.

Page 73
Prayer: Quick & Dirty began as a very small artist book of drawings, found text and torn paper. With many thanks to Deborah Faeryglenn for gifting that blank micro journal with its zingy orange cover.

Page 84
Kids Half Price is an erasure poem derived from 'People smuggling — Turkey, Greece exodus,' accessed 24 November 2016. <https://www.theguardian.com/tv-and-radio/2016/jul/07/people-smuggling-turkey-greece-exodus-bbc-tv-documentary>

Page 85

Syria's Children is an ekphrastic sequence written in response to the moving photo-story sequence by award winning photojournalist Magnum Wennman titled *Where the Children Sleep* published at *Mashable Australia*. With great thanks. <http://mashable.com/2015/10/02/where-the-children-sleep/?utm_cid=mash-com-fb-main-link#t7Bbl2hWY5qn>

acknowledgements

The new writing in *The Wear of My Face* and development of the overall manuscript would not have been possible without support from the ACT Government, for which I cannot show enough appreciation.

Some poems were previously published in: *Aesthetica Creative Writing Annual* (UK), ArtSound FM, *Australian Love Poems* (ed. Mark Tredinnick, Inkerman & Blunt 2013), *Australian Poetry Anthology* 2020 (AP), *Award Winning Australian Writing* (ed. Adolfo Arunjuez, Melbourne Books 2012), *Backstory Journal, The Canberra Times, FourXFour* (Ireland), *Not Very Quiet* (Issue 6, 2020; Issue 8, 2021), *Other Terrain Journal, Rochford Street Review, Social Alternatives, These Strange Outcrops: Writing and Art from Canberra* (*Cicerone Journal*'s Canberra Writing Anthology Project 2020), *Verity La.*

The Architecture of Pear won the Rosemary Dobson Poetry Prize 2011; *Prayer: Quick & Dirty* was Highly Commended in the Blake Poetry Prize 2013; *A Woman's Work* was shortlisted in Aesthetica Creative Writing Award (UK) 2014.

Brown Goshawk is included in the music and spoken word audio recording accompanying the touring exhibition *Bimblebox: 153 Birds* <https://bimbleboxartproject.com> coordinated by Jill Sampson, to promote awareness of the Bimblebox Nature Reserve in Queensland, under threat from coal mining. *The Power of Prayer* is included in *Kindred Trees* <http://kindredtrees.com.au> a project promoting the love of trees through poetry in Canberra and beyond, instigated by Sarah St Vincent Welch.

A number of poems had their beginnings in *Project 366* coordinated by Kit Kelen <https://project365plus.blogspot.com/> or in *Postcards from the Sky* an ongoing living studio project/collective supported by Belconnen Arts Centre and Artistic Director/Co-CEO Moni McInerney. I am grateful to all these poets and artists. Love also to Yass Valley poets Jane Baker, Victoria McGrath and Robyn Sykes for their wenchie friendship and Merlinda Bobis, Kathy Kituai and Jenni Kemarre Martiniello for Blissmaking.

Thank you to all those who, unwittingly or otherwise, provided creative spark for individual poems including: Merlinda Bobis, Moyra Donaldson, Marianne Boruch, the late Richard Conrick, Peter Crisp, Wayne Dawe, Deborah Faeryglenn, Elena Garcia and my bro Stretch Jamison, Glenyse Ings, Chris Mansell, Jenni Kemarre Martiniello, Kathleen McCracken, Asha Naznin, Janene Pellarin, Heather and Hilary Sharwood, Sarah St Vincent Welch, David Terelinck, Robert Verdon. Another vote of love to beekeepers Glenyse and Bob Ings, Susan Morrissey and Helen White for added buzz. Most special thanks to my dear Bill, Aroona and Brendan — always an inspiration.

Immense thanks in particular to: Merlinda Bobis, Marianne Boruch and Sarah St Vincent Welch for invaluable support and advice; Camilla Duffy for capturing photography; Susan Hawthorne for enlightening editing; designer Deb Snibson and typesetter and designer Helen Christie for exquisite cover and page design; the whole Spinifex team for bringing women's writing to the world.

I am indebted to publishers Susan Hawthorne and Renate Klein and thrilled to be published during the 30th Anniversary year of Spinifex Press.

Other books by Lizz Murphy

Two Lips Went Shopping

Two huge lips went shopping
on a pogo stick
for a red satin handbag
coordinated in colour
with their cupid's bow

This is a book for anyone who has ever shopped — or worked in shops. But whether you find yourself wincing or laughing could depend on which side of the shop counter you're on at the time.

Spirited, cheeky and angst-free … the poetry is unrhymed drawing pleasure from the rhythm and feel of language … her best poems remodel the everyday to recast the familiar and frustrating with witty flair.

—Mike Shuttleworth, *The Sunday Age*

ISBN: 9781875559961

Wee Girls: Women Writing from an Irish Perspective

A moving and often amusing collection of fiction, poetry and autobiography by top-selling and award-winning authors. Tales of blood and bloodlines — Irish grandmothers, ma's and da's, the Famine and the Troubles. Whatever the form, these are the stories, the music, the whispering dreams and the voices that ache to be heard. There is wildness and daring in these voices. They call up legions out of the sea and set fires alight. They hang out over garden fences, move restlessly, are dotey, beaming, weeping, powerful.

… it is simply worth reading because the writing is resoundingly good.

—Veronica Gleeson, *Ariel View*

ISBN: 9781875559510

Other poetry titles from Spinifex Press

Accidents of Composition

Merlinda Bobis

Highly Commended, ACT Book of the Year Award

The eyes catch a black bird close to an eerie sun. Instantly, a poem: an accident of composition. Or a tree, rock, light from a story heard, dreamt, read or remembered returns as if it were the only tree, rock, light in the planet. The poet is caught, returned to her first heart: poetry.

… a collection expansive and transitory in its various vantage points. The poems traverse diverse times and spaces: global and intimate, historical and mythical. They elicit — and are imbued with — humour, compassion and moments of disquietude.

—Jo Langdon, *Sydney Review of Books*

ISBN: 9781742199986

The Abbotsford Mysteries

Patricia Sykes

The Abbotsford Convent becomes more than the setting, *the grey mince-meat walls*, of this collection. It emerges as presence, intimate and familiar as well as constraining and forbidding. But it is childhood itself which becomes the subterranean geography and pulse.

Not just a setting, the Abbotsford Convent is home to orphan girls, 'wayward' girls and country girls, as well as the nuns who care for them. The voices in these poems pulse with memory as religious and lay people share their memories of institutionalised life.

Spirited and fugitive, lively and resistant … These are moving compassionate poems full of the motif of river: life, undercurrent, debris — and the deeply aspiring self.

—Philip Salom

ISBN: 9781876756956

between wind and water (in a vulnerable place)

berni m janssen

between wind and water, a series of poems, tells the stories of people who, after a windfarm is built in their neighbourhood, find that they begin to experience problems: among others sleep disruption, headaches, nausea, anxiety. They complain to the Company, local council, and government. Lost in the labyrinth of doublespeak and duplicity, anxiety, disillusionment and a sense of abandonment grow.

Rejoice! berni janssen's new book! This book is easy to love: its rugged, soft, deft, exact forms. Action is embedded in things; politics is stitched into the wind. Set against the bamboozle clatter of corpspeak and co-option. It's a beautifully grounded book and it's going to make trouble.

—Chris Mansell, Poet and Publisher

ISBN: 9781925581591

This Intimate War: Gallipoli/Çanakkale 1915: İçli Dışlı Bir Savaş: Gelibolu/Çanakkale 1915

Robyn Rowland AO
Turkish translations by Dr Mehmet Ali Çelikel

'Very few collections bring home so powerfully the vulnerability of individuals in the face of history' writes Lisa Gorton of Robyn Rowland's powerful poems recording the experiences of soldiers, nurses and doctors, women munitions workers, wives, mothers, composers, painters and poets during the Gallipoli War, 1915.

Stories of Australian, Turkish and Irish men and women in these poems show the intimate nature of war; not from the perspective of victory but from the perspective of those caught up in war, who, whichever side they were on, lost.

—Lisa Gorton, author of *Empirical*

ISBN: 9781925581386

The Mad Poet's Tea Party

Sandy Jeffs OAM

Sandy Jeffs shares her journey through madness over four decades, drawing inspiration from Lewis Carroll's *Alice In Wonderland*, managing to be whimsical and witty while also providing a devastating commentary on how society treats those with mental illness.

I never imagined describing madness could be so rich, so vivid and so full of humour ...

—Meryl Tankard

It's clear poetry is Jeffs's world; it permeates ordinary human existence, doing its best to withstand insanity and capitalism.

—Michael Farrell, *The Australian*

ISBN: 9781742199498

Dark Matter: New Poems

Robin Morgan

In this major new book of poems, her seventh, Robin Morgan rewards us with the award-winning mastery we've come to expect from her poetry. Her gaze is unflinching, her craft sharp, her mature voice rich with wry wit, survived pain, and her signature chord: an indomitable celebration of life. This powerful collection contains the now-famous poems Morgan reads in her TED Talk — viewed online more than a million times and translated into 24 languages.

FIVE STARS. This collection read like one long glorious, insightful and playful reflection and celebration of life, love, friendship and death. Read by Morgan as a TED Talk and viewed online more than a million times ... I'm not surprised.

—Sally Piper, author, *GoodReads*

ISBN: 9781925581430

An Embroidery of Old Maps and New

Angela Costi

Migration and the memories of women's traditions are woven throughout these poems. Angela Costi brings the world of Cyprus to Australia. Her mother encounters animosity on Melbourne's trams as Angela learns to thread words in ways that echo her grandmother's embroidery. Here are poems that sing their way across the seas and map histories.

These powerful, poignant poems embody the experience of generations of women, the dignity of their labour, their affirmation of life as a journey into uncharted realms, where they must adapt their skills to sustain their children in an unfamiliar culture: a challenge to be embraced wholeheartedly, bodily.
—Jena Woodhouse, author of *News from the Village: Travels in Rural Greece*

ISBN: 9781925950243

I Will Not Bear You Sons

Usha Akella

A poem can glisten like a fresh wound.

Usha Akella pays tribute to the lives of women from cultures across continents, while reflecting on her own life. Her poems are the medium for women who refuse to be silenced. She condenses a calm rage into ferocious words of precision and celebrates the women who have triumphed. All the while a subversive dusting of humour runs through the collection.

We are truly at precipice and this poetry can help wake up the world to itself. Kudos.
—Anne Waldman, author of *Trickster Feminism*

ISBN: 9781925950281

If you would like to know more about Spinifex Press,
visit our website and subscribe to our newsletter,
or email us for further information.

Spinifex Press
PO Box 105
Mission Beach QLD 4852
Australia

www.spinifexpress.com.au
women@spinifexpress.com.au